YOU CHOOSE™
BOOKS
Historical Eras

The Aztec Empire

An Interactive History Adventure

by Elizabeth Raum

Consultant:
Colin M. MacLachlan, PhD
History Department
Tulane University

Raintree is an imprint of Capstone Global Library Limited, a company incorporated in
England and Wales having its registered office at 7 Pilgrim Street, London, EC4V 6LB –
Registered company number: 6695582

www.raintreepublishers.co.uk
myorders@raintreepublishers.co.uk

Text © Capstone Global Library Limited 2015
The moral rights of the proprietor have been asserted.

ISBN 978 1 474 70649 0
19 18 17 16 15
10 9 8 7 6 5 4 3 2 1

Printed and bound in China

British Library Cataloguing in Publication Data
A full catalogue record for this book is available from the British Library.

Photo Credits
Alamy: North Wind Picture Archives, 6, 60, 70, Ruslan Bustamante, 100; Art Resource, N.Y.:
Werner Forman, 96; Bridgeman Art Library International/Private Collection/Stephen Reid,
80; Capstone: Carl Lyons, 10, 68; Corbis: Bettmann, 38, 67, 88, National Geographic Stock/H.
Tom Hall, cover; Dreamstime: Czuber, 17; National Geographic Stock: Felipe Dávalos 52;
Rourke Publishing, LLC: How They Lived: An Aztec Warrior, 40; SuperStock Inc: dieKleinert,
46; www.mexicolore.co.uk: 24, 28, Felipe Dávalos, 12, 32, Ian Mursell, 55

TABLE OF CONTENTS

About your ADVENTURE

YOU are living on the island of Tenochtitlan in the Valley of Mexico around the 15th century. The Aztec people of the island are brave, creative, and intelligent. But European conquistadors are moving in. What will happen to the Aztecs and their way of life?

In this book you'll explore how the choices people made meant the difference between life and death. The events you'll experience happened to real people.

Chapter one sets the scene. Then you choose which path to read. Follow the directions at the bottom of each page. The choices you make will change your outcome. After you finish your path, go back and read the others for new perspectives and more adventures.

*YOU CHOOSE the path
you take through history.*

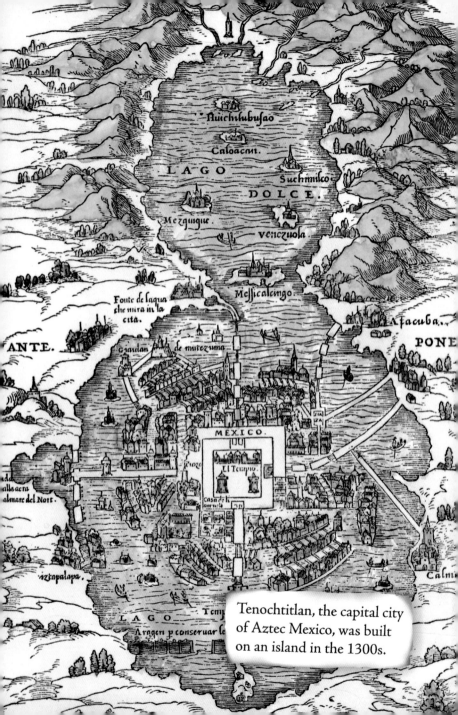

Tenochtitlan, the capital city of Aztec Mexico, was built on an island in the 1300s.

City of dreams

The Aztec people founded one of the most powerful empires in history. The Aztecs, who were also called the Mexica, lived in Atzlan. Atzlan was located somewhere in northern Mexico or the southwestern United States. In about 1100, the Mexica left Atzlan and worked their way south for more than 200 years. They reached Mexico's Central Valley and settled on an island in Lake Texcoco in 1325. There they began building the great city of Tenochtitlan.

They built temples and pyramids in the city centre. These buildings rose high above the streets and canals of the island. Stone serpent heads guarded the pyramids. Nearby were large villas that belonged to wealthy nobles. There were gardens, fountains, and even zoos.

Turn the page.

Aztec workers lived farther from the city centre. Five or six adobe huts shared a courtyard where people cooked and visited. Neighbourhoods were organized by jobs.

Carpenters lived in one neighbourhood. Potters and basket makers lived in others. Farmers planted crops and flowers along the shoreline or on man-made islands called chinampas. Aztec traders kept the city supplied with goods of all kinds.

The Aztecs fought wars nearly all the time. They captured nearby cities and towns, not to destroy them, but to claim their riches. Captured towns had to pay tributes to Tenochtitlan. These tributes might be crops, cloth, or precious metals such as gold and silver.

Aztec warriors also took captives. Some captured enemies were used as slaves for a while. But eventually, all captives were sacrificed to the Aztec gods. The Aztecs believed that the gods created people from their own blood. They repaid the gods with human sacrifices.

Every Aztec boy trained to be a warrior. A few became lifelong soldiers, but most also learned other trades such as farming, carpentry, or jewellery making. Girls learned weaving and embroidery. They created beautiful cloaks worn by nobles. Some girls became teachers, healers, or judges in the marketplace. Between ages 12 and 15, Aztec teens attended schools to learn religious songs and dances.

Turn the page.

By 1500, between 200,000 and 300,000 people lived in Tenochtitlan. It was the world's largest city. The great market in Tlatelolco was located just north of Tenochtitlan on the same island. As many as 50,000 people shopped there daily. Market stalls were divided by type, so that all flower sellers were in one place while vendors offering hot tamales and other foods were in another.

The Aztecs traded goods at the market in Tlatelolco, near Tenochtitlan.

The high mountains of central Mexico not only provided timber and water, but they also were rich with gold. Aztec metalworkers created beautiful golden jewellery, statues, and other objects. When Spanish conquistador Hernán Cortés first arrived in Tenochtitlan, he called it a "city of dreams".

Cortés dreamed of gold. He found it – and more – in Tenochtitlan. What will you find when you visit Tenochtitlan?

➡To experience life as a merchant's daughter during the middle of the 1400s when the Aztec Empire is growing and expanding, turn to page **13**.

➡To experience life as the son of a nobleman during the late 1400s when the Aztec Empire is reaching its peak, turn to page **39**.

➡To experience life as a page under the command of Cortés in the early 1500s, turn to page **71**.

The market at Tlatelolco was the centre of commerce for the Aztec empire.

CHAPTER 2

Aztec girl

"Wait, Zyanya," you call as your cousin races ahead of you towards the market. "We're not children anymore."

Zyanya waits for you to catch up. You make a point of walking slowly, swaying your hips from side to side so that your long skirt swirls around your legs. Your hair, which is nearly shoulder length, swishes as you walk. Now that you are both 12, your mothers have stopped cutting your hair short like a boy's.

13

Turn the page.

It doesn't take long to reach the great market at Tlatelolco. Auntie Chantico, Zyanya's mother, sells cloaks there. Mother is a marketplace judge. Mother's job is to make sure prices are fair. If disagreements arise, she helps settle them.

You pass rows of market stalls. Everything you could want or need is for sale there – cloth and thread of all colours, pottery, jewellery, meat such as rabbit, deer, or gopher, and even tasty pastries. Thousands of shoppers bargain for goods. There is much trading, and some people use cacao beans or turkey quills filled with gold dust as money. In one row, jewellers sell necklaces of turquoise, silver, and gold.

You stop to look at the earplugs of clay, bone, and seashell. Your ears were pierced during the stretching ceremony when you were 4 years old. The holes were tiny then, but you've stretched them so they are almost big enough for adult earplugs.

At last you reach the street where Auntie Chantico sells her beautiful embroidered cloaks. Her prices are high, but her cloaks are the best.

"Please watch the stall while I do an errand. I am depending on you to make good bargains," she says to you and Zyanya as she rushes away.

Turn the page.

You finger the soft cotton cloaks. Some are pure white. Others are bright red, dipped in dye made from the cochineal bugs that live on the prickly pear cactus. Your father brought these cloaks home from his last trading journey. Auntie sells them for him. Father brings home other treasures too. The best go to the emperor, the great Montezuma.

A woman holds up a white cloak covered with delicate embroidery. "I will give you 300 cacao beans for this cloak," she says. It is a good bargain.

You pull your cousin aside. Something about the way the woman is smiling worries you.

"She doesn't look honest," you say.

"You decide," Zyanya says.

➤To sell the cloak to the woman, go to page 17.

➤To refuse her offer, turn to page 19.

You go ahead with the sale. When Auntie Chantico returns, you show her the cacao beans. She selects one and pulls it apart. "It's fake," she says. "The chocolate has been removed from the outer husk and replaced with sand."

Cacao beans were used as money to purchase goods and services.

Turn the page.

About half the beans are bad, but the woman has long since disappeared. "You will learn," your aunt says gently.

That evening as you are eating together in the courtyard, your mother says, "Mistakes happen when you are learning. Many people have been fooled. It is my job to remove dishonest traders from the marketplace and report them to the authorities. Would you like to become a marketplace judge like me? Or perhaps you'd rather be a healer. Your Aunt Nenetl will train you to help the sick as she does."

➼To become a healer, turn to page **21**.

➼To train as a marketplace judge, turn to page **22**.

You refuse the woman's offer. When Auntie Chantico returns, she is disappointed. Later, you tell your mother what happened. Mother nods. "The woman's offer was too generous. Some thieves remove the chocolate from the cacao beans and fill the husk with sand. A trader must be alert. It was wise to refuse what seemed like too good an offer."

Mother's basket is overflowing with fresh game meat – frogs, ducks, and a gopher. "Is Father coming home?" you ask.

Mother nods. "Yes, a runner brought the news. We must prepare a fine welcome."

Father is often gone for months at a time on trading trips. When he left, you asked the gods to protect him. His safe return means that your prayers have been answered.

Turn the page.

The homecoming celebrations continue for two days. Father tells of gathering quetzal feathers from traders far to the south. "The emperor will be pleased," Father says, holding up glittery red and green feathers. Father has also brought pottery, jewellery, and more beautiful cloaks for Auntie to sell.

A few days after Father's return, your parents ask if you are ready to begin training with Mother to be a judge in the marketplace. "Or," Father says, "you can continue to work with Auntie Chantico selling the cloaks I've brought home from my trading mission."

→To become a judge, turn to page **22**.

→To help Auntie sell cloaks, turn to page **27**.

It is exciting to learn about medicines from Aunt Nenetl. She teaches you how to make salve from the prickly pear cactus. It eases pain, helps burns to heal, and prevents wounds from becoming red and swollen. She teaches you about other plants and medicines.

One day you are preparing herbs when a small boy rushes in. "Come and help us, please! My brother has fallen into the fire and burned his legs." Your aunt is visiting another neighbourhood. If not treated properly, the boy might die.

➛ To search for your aunt, turn to page 25.

➛ To help the injured boy, turn to page 29.

You follow Mother through the marketplace. Will you ever be as wise as she is? She teaches you the difference between good cacao beans and poor ones. She makes sure that vendors charge fair prices. When an argument breaks out between two women selling maize, Mother steps in and settles the fight.

Soon after you turn 15, a matchmaker visits your parents. A young man named Necalli wants to marry you. Necalli is 21. He's a merchant like your father, and he's handsome and smart.

At first your parents refuse the matchmaker's offer. They don't want to appear too eager. If they refuse, you will seem an even better catch. The third time the matchmaker asks, your parents agree.

Necalli's parents choose a wedding date that will bring luck. At sunset on the chosen day, your mother and aunts bathe you with soap and sprinkle your face with red and yellow ochre. Then Necalli's family carries you to their home. You sit on a reed mat before the hearth. Necalli joins you.

Necalli's mother brings you a new dress called a huipilli. Your mother gives Necalli a new cape. The matchmaker steps forward and ties a corner of Necalli's cape to your huipilli. Once she has tied the knot, you are married. Now you will begin a new life together.

Turn the page.

Girls typically married between the ages of 15 and 18. Boys were usually several years older.

You move in with Necalli's parents. After the wedding, Necalli and his father leave on a trading mission. "While I am away, you must keep busy," Necalli says. "That way you will not miss me as much. Perhaps you can return to the marketplace and work with your mother. Or you can weave cloaks. I will sell them when I return."

➤To weave cloaks, turn to page **31**.

➤To return to work with your mother, turn to page **33**.

24

"I will get my aunt," you say. "She will know what to do."

You race through the streets to find Aunt Nenetl, but by the time you both reach the boy's home, he is dead. Aunt kneels beside the small body and examines his burns. She shakes her head. "Had we treated him quickly, he might have lived. Next time you must not wait for me. Trust yourself. You are a healer."

It is high praise, but her words only add to your guilt. You should have gone directly to help the boy.

Turn the page.

As you are leaving, the family begins preparing the small body for its journey to Mictlan, the Land of the Dead. They wash him, wrap him in a cloth with some favourite items, and burn his body. Later, they'll bury his ashes beneath the floor of the house.

You cannot sleep that night. It's your fault the boy died. The next morning you speak to Aunt Nenetl. "I will help you grow herbs and prepare medicines," you say, "but you must find someone else to care for the sick and injured."

Aunt Nenetl reassures you. "We cannot save everyone. It is up to the gods who lives or dies. Please continue this good work."

→To continue working with the sick, turn to page 34.

→To make medicines, turn to page 35.

You admire Mother's work as a judge, but you'd rather work as a merchant. After all, you were born under the ninth sign, One Serpent. It is a special sign for merchants. No wonder you were able to spot the fake cacao beans.

A few years after you've begun working, a matchmaker arrives to speak with Father. It is time for you to marry. At first your parents refuse the matchmaker. This makes you seem even more valuable to your future husband. But after some time, they agree that you will marry Tupac. Although he is not yet 23, he has taken two captives in battle. It is an honour to be married to a brave warrior.

When Tupac is not at war, he is a goldsmith like his father. He makes bells and beautiful gold jewellery. After your wedding, you move in with Tupac's family.

Turn the page.

Women wove with imported cotton or with fibres from the maguey plant.

A few weeks later, Tupac leaves for battle. Every evening while he is gone, you weave. The new cloak will be a surprise when he returns home.

One rainy day a few weeks later, Zyanya rushes over to tell you that a runner has returned with news of the battle.

➤To meet the runner, turn to page **36**.

➤To wait until he reaches your neighbourhood, turn to page **37**.

"Hurry!" the boy says. You grab some medicine and dash after him.

The injured brother lies in the courtyard beside the fire. He is unconscious. Burns cover much of his lower body.

"I need wet cloths," you say. The family runs to get what you need. You apply the cloths to the burns, cooling the boy's skin. You then cover his legs with salve made from the prickly pear cactus. "You must let him rest," you say. "I will be back to check on him."

When Aunt Nenetl returns, she visits the boy. "You have done well," she tells you. "He might have died from such a serious injury."

Turn the page.

You work with your aunt for several months, learning how to make medicines from plants and herbs. Sometimes you go to market to buy rare plants. Many others grow in Aunt's garden. People begin coming directly to you for help. Aunt doesn't mind. She is getting older and is happy to turn the work over to you.

In a few years' time, you marry and settle into a home of your own. Over the years, your special talent as a healer brings you the respect of your community.

30

THE END

To follow another path, turn to page 11.
To read the conclusion, turn to page 101.

Like all girls, you learned weaving from your mother at an early age. You find working with cloth peaceful, and you enjoy the long hours sitting at the loom. By the time Necalli returns from his trading mission, you have several cloaks ready for him to sell.

When you become pregnant, the entire family celebrates. They treat you like a queen. Becoming a mother is the most important role in an Aztec woman's life. A midwife helps you during childbirth. She has been present at many births, and it is her job to welcome the baby into the world.

"It is a girl," she cries as the baby is born.

Turn the page.

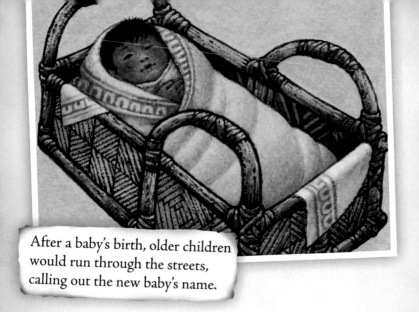

After a baby's birth, older children would run through the streets, calling out the new baby's name.

When your little girl is 4 days old, the midwife carries the naked child into the courtyard, bathes her, and names her Tlalli. Family and neighbours bring Tlalli gifts – a tiny spindle for weaving and a broom. These gifts reflect the roles she will play as an adult. Someday you will teach Tlalli to use them. But for now, you celebrate her safe arrival with 20 days of feasting.

THE END

To follow another path, turn to page 11.
To read the conclusion, turn to page 101.

Mother is grateful for your help in the marketplace.

Necalli returns in three months and quickly sells his wares. "I must go to get more items to sell," he says. "I'll be home again soon."

But this time Necalli doesn't return. Enemy warriors captured him near the coast. You know that a man as young and beautiful as Necalli will be sacrificed to the gods. Your sadness is overwhelming. You can't stop crying.

Perhaps you will marry again. But with so many young men killed or captured in battle, you may not find another husband. You still have your work, though. For now, that will have to be enough.

THE END

To follow another path, turn to page 11.
To read the conclusion, turn to page 101.

You agree to try again. You watch as Aunt Nenetl helps people with stomach aches, headaches, and skin rashes. When you mend a small girl's broken arm, Aunt Nenetl says, "You were born to be a healer."

You later marry and have a family of your own. But you continue to care for sick and injured people, following in your aunt's footsteps.

THE END

To follow another path, turn to page 11.
To read the conclusion, turn to page 101.

"I will make medicines," you say. As your skills improve, Aunt Nenetl says, "Now I have more time to treat patients." Your cousin Zyanya opens her own stall at the market selling the lotions and creams that you make.

Soon after you turn 16, you marry a farmer named Matlal. You have bought herbs from him. Now you will move to his farm and begin your own family. "You can still make medicines," Aunt reminds you. But you are busy keeping house, raising children, and helping Matlal with the farm work. You don't forget the skills your aunt taught you, though. You use them to keep your family healthy.

35

THE END

To follow another path, turn to page 11.
To read the conclusion, turn to page 101.

You're eager to hear the news. Even though the streets are slick with rain, you dash towards the city centre, slipping and sliding as you run. There's just one last canal to cross. The boards that form a footbridge over the canal are slippery.

You're fine until you reach the middle of the footbridge. Then you slip and break your arm. You hit the water feet first. "Help me!" you call. You can't swim with an injured arm. But no one comes. As you sink below the surface, your last thoughts are of Tupac. Did he survive the battle? You'll never know. You drown in the cool waters of Lake Texcoco.

THE END

To follow another path, turn to page 11.
To read the conclusion, turn to page 101.

Married women should not run through the streets. The news will reach you soon enough.

When Tupac reaches home, his face is painted red and yellow.

"You have taken another captive?" you ask.

He nods. That makes three in total. He's a hero. Now he will attend war councils. Perhaps soon he will become a military officer. You are proud of your husband and eager to become the mother of his children.

THE END

To follow another path, turn to page 11.
To read the conclusion, turn to page 101.

Jaguar knights and other elite warriors wore elaborate costumes to battle.

CHAPTER 3

Noble youth

Soon after your 10th birthday, Father says, "Next week you will begin attending school for warrior training. Don't be lazy!"

He watches as your head is shaved. One tuft at the back will be your nape lock. You won't cut it until you have captured an enemy warrior.

You work hard studying the history of your people and how to govern. You learn songs and dances that please the gods. You also spend time working in the palace gardens and studying landscaping. Everyone agrees that you have a talent for it. Perhaps when you are too old to fight on the battlefield, you'll design palace gardens. It is a noble profession.

Turn the page.

By the time you are 15, you have earned the respect of the other students. Now you will begin weapons training. You will soon be going to war.

First you learn to use projectile weapons, such as bows and arrows, slings, and spear throwers. Usually commoners use these weapons, but even noble warriors must master them.

The telpochcalli was the school that taught military arts and other trades.

You also practise using an arrow launcher called an atlatl. It looks like a stick with a notch at one end. A dart is placed into a groove carved along the atlatl's length. The notch holds it in place. When the warrior makes a throwing motion, the dart sails towards the enemy. It takes practice to throw the dart accurately.

Today you'll practise with shock weapons, which are used in close combat. One group of students will be trained on the two-handed sword called the macuahuitl. It has sharp cutting edges made of obsidian, a volcanic glass. The other group will learn to use the tepoztopilli, a thrusting spear.

➤ *To use the macuahuitl, turn to page 42.*
➤ *To use the tepoztopilli, turn to page 44.*

A successful warrior named Zolton teaches you how to use the macuahuitl.

"Careful," Zolton says. "The obsidian blades running along both sides are sharp."

"It is a deadly weapon," he continues. "But your job is not to kill the enemy. You must capture him alive." Killing an enemy may save your life, but capturing him alive will bring you honour.

By the time you are 18, you have mastered this weapon and many others. It is time to observe battle firsthand.

As you prepare to go to war, your friend Luc asks if you are afraid.

"No," you say quickly. "To die in battle is an honour." You have been taught that death on the battlefield brings great reward. For four years after you die, you will follow the sun across the sky from morning to noon. Then you will return to earth as a butterfly or hummingbird.

"A great honour," Luc agrees, "but perhaps we should continue to practise."

➤To practise, turn to page **45**.

➤To rest before battle, turn to page **46**.

You join the group training on the tepoztopilli. "You don't throw it," the instructor says. "You thrust it at the enemy, crippling him so that he surrenders. Taking captives will bring you honour."

You continue to practise with various weapons – the bow and arrow, knife, atlatl, and of course, the tepoztopilli. Hard physical labour prepares your body for battle. At last, when you turn 18, you are allowed to observe a battle.

Your father will pay a seasoned warrior to take you under his care. He asks if you prefer an Eagle Knight or a Jaguar Knight. Jaguar and Eagle Knights are members of elite military orders. They've proven themselves in battle.

➤ To go with an Eagle Knight, turn to page **48**.

➤ To go with a Jaguar Knight, turn to page **52**.

"Let's practise," you say, heading for a hidden corner of the courtyard.

You hold a shield before your face as protection. Luc slashes the air with his macuahuitl. He will not harm you, at least not on purpose. But he is tired. At the last minute, he lets go. The macuahuitl flies at you!

You leap backwards, tripping over a rock and twisting your leg. You cry out in pain.

"I'll get help," Luc calls.

"No, wait!" You worry that if your teachers discover that you are injured, you won't be allowed to go to battle. Maybe you should see if the leg heals itself in the next few days.

➤To wait for the leg to heal, turn to page **65**.

➤To summon a healer, turn to page **66**.

You decide against more practice. Your father arranges for you to go to battle with Coatl, a man of great courage. You will carry his weapons and supplies to the battlefield.

On the day you march to battle, you meet at sunrise. "You'll watch the battle from the hillside," Coatl says. From your high-up place, you see the two armies approach one another. When they are about 4.5 metres (15 feet) apart, the archers release their arrows.

Warriors tried to take as many captives as possible during hand-to-hand combat.

When they run out of arrows, warriors with atlatls send darts at the enemy. It only takes a few minutes to fire the projectiles. Then the archers run to safety. Now the elite warriors begin hand-to-hand combat. You hear the thud of spears against wooden shields. Battle cries fill the air.

The fighting doesn't last long. There are many captives.

You return to Tenochtitlan with the triumphant warriors and the doomed captives. Emperor Ahuitzotl is pleased. All of Tenochtitlan celebrates. A few days later, the captives are sacrificed to the god of the sun and war.

Your father is proud. He asks you if you are ready to marry.

➤To marry, turn to page **56**.

➤To wait, turn to page **57**.

"I'd like to be an Eagle Knight someday," you say. Your father chooses an Eagle Knight named Coatl to guide you during the first battle. You carry his supplies and prepare his food during the long march to battle.

War does not happen by surprise. Ambassadors from Tenochtitlan have pleaded with a neighbouring city to pay tribute to your emperor, Ahuitzotl. But they would rather fight than give in to the mighty Tenochtitlan ruler.

And so the battle begins. First archers and dart throwers hurl projectiles at the enemy. The enemy warriors shoot arrows and darts back at your warriors. The weapons thud against the wooden shields. Then the best warriors enter the battle. You watch from the hillside, eager for the day when you can join the fight.

The battle won, you return in triumph to Tenochtitlan. You go to the temple to watch the sacrifice of captives. Some must be pushed up the pyramid stairs. Others walk bravely to their deaths. The crowd cheers as the priest rips the heart from a captive's chest and lifts it up to the sun god.

You meet friends at the temple. "Come with us," they say. "We will celebrate." One of the boys, Tenoch, has pulque, a kind of beer that farmers and city workers drink.

"It is against the rules," you say. "If someone finds out…"

"No one will ever know," Tenoch says.

→To join them, turn to page **50**.

→To return to school, turn to page **54**.

You wander through the streets with Tenoch, but when he offers you a drink, you refuse. "Public drunkenness is punishable by death," you warn, but Tenoch only scoffs.

No matter what you say, Tenoch answers with teasing words. You're tired of his teasing. "I'll see you tomorrow," you say, as you return to the school.

It is two days before you see one of the boys who had been drinking the pulque. He walks with a limp, and his ears are bleeding.

"What happened?" you ask.

"One of the instructors caught us with pulque. I was beaten and pierced with maguey spines," he says. "Tenoch nearly died of his beating. He has been thrown out of the school permanently."

You're very glad you returned to the school when you did.

Your teachers announce that another war is near. Coatl encourages you. "This is your chance to take a captive. Be confident."

It takes a few days to reach the battlefield. Despite Coatl's encouraging words, you don't feel confident. The battle is about to begin. You must decide whether to step forward or not.

➔ To fight, turn to page **60**.

➔ To watch, turn to page **68**.

Your older brother, Xipilli, is a Jaguar Knight. He will be your guide in battle. He insists that you observe the first battle from a distance. By the second battle, you are ready to join the attack.

"Choose someone your age," Xipilli says. "You'll have a better chance that way. Remember, the goal is not to kill – it is to capture the enemy. That will please the emperor and the gods."

Jaguar Knights wore jaguar skins. Eagle Knights wore feathers.

Noise surrounds you. Weapons clunk against wooden shields. Warriors shout out the names of their towns. From time to time, a warrior screams as he falls wounded. You find a warrior who looks about your age. He's alone in an area away from the main battle. You sneak forward, your shield in one hand and your spear in the other.

As you close in, your heart races and your hand sweats as it grips the polished wood of your weapon. You lunge at your enemy. At the same moment, he lunges towards you. Your spear bounces off his shield, but his hits its mark. Your shoulder burns where the blade struck.

➤To drop your weapon, turn to page **62**.

➤To strike again, turn to page **64**.

You return to school and prepare for the next battle. You practise many hours with your weapons. You study warfare and talk to experienced warriors. You even cut your ears with maguey thorns until they bleed. Such sacrifices please the gods.

This time you will fight. As a new warrior, you cannot wear body armour or paint your face. All you have is a shield to protect you. You carry a knife and the tepoztopilli. Your teachers said that you may work with five or six other new warriors for your first capture.

The commander sounds the conch shell. The battle is on. Arrows and darts fly through the air. As the archers retreat, skilled warriors take the field. At last it is time for you to advance. Your friends are waiting for you to join them for a group capture.

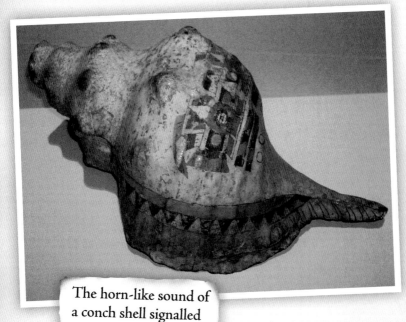

The horn-like sound of a conch shell signalled the start of a battle.

➺To join them, turn to page **59**.

➺To act alone, turn to page **60**.

"Yes, I want to marry." Your parents consult your teachers and relatives to find a suitable bride. Then they hire a matchmaker to approach the girl's parents. You won't meet the girl until your wedding day.

Your bride, Atzi, is of noble birth, and she's lovely. Atzi moves into your father's palace to begin married life.

Your mother is pleased by the prospect of grandchildren. You're eager to have a family, but you also look forward to returning to the battlefield. You will bring honour to your family and your emperor.

THE END

To follow another path, turn to page 11.
To read the conclusion, turn to page 101.

You are still young. You ask your father's permission to wait before marrying. First you want to make your mark as a great warrior.

In a first battle, young warriors may team up to take a captive. When the day of your first battle arrives, you join five other new warriors and successfully capture an enemy. When you return to the city, the emperor calls you to the palace. Now that you have proved yourself, you cut your nape lock.

During the next battle, you take a captive on your own. When you are taken to see the emperor, your face is painted red. The emperor's tribute collectors add yellow paint to your temples. From now on you may wear warrior's clothing even during peacetime.

Turn the page.

As your family celebrates the victory, you tell them that you are ready to marry. Because you come from a royal family, your father arranges a royal marriage. You will marry the daughter of the king whose city you helped to conquer. Someday your son will become the leader there. He will bring honour to the empire as you have done.

THE END

To follow another path, turn to page 11.
To read the conclusion, turn to page 101.

There is strength in numbers. Your group moves on to the battlefield. "There," one of them shouts. He points to a lone enemy warrior, not much older than you are.

When you are within reach, you lash out, striking his knee. He strikes back, but the others help you overpower him. He cries out and gives up.

Men with ropes rush forward, taking your captive to the rear.

You return to the city rejoicing. Because you have taken a captive, you cut your nape lock and paint your face. Now you are a man. You'll soon earn the rank of Eagle Knight.

THE END

To follow another path, turn to page 11.
To read the conclusion, turn to page 101.

You step onto the battlefield alone and choose your opponent. You prepare to thrust the tepoztopilli at him, but he manages to strike first. You collapse and fall to the ground. Your enemy stands over you, ready to strike again. You have no choice but to surrender.

An Aztec priest prepares for a sacrifice.

You know what awaits – your death as a sacrifice to the gods. Capturing an enemy brings honour. Death on the battlefield brings honour. But death as a captive brings only sorrow and pain.

Two days later, you are marched to the pyramid. The man ahead of you faints, but you remain strong as you climb to the top of the pyramid. Several priests are waiting. They grab you and lower you to a stone table. The last thing you see is the obsidian knife high in the air above your heart.

THE END

To follow another path, turn to page 11.
To read the conclusion, turn to page 101.

You drop your weapon and sink to the ground, expecting to become a captive. But Xipilli slips in beside you. He strikes out, knocking down the enemy and taking him captive.

You lie on the ground, clutching your wounded shoulder. Men rush onto the field to tie up the enemy captive, and Xipilli moves on. A priest washes your wound and applies a salve made of healing herbs and plants. Then he bandages it with a clean cloth. You will survive, although your arm is severely damaged. Despite your pain, you're glad that your army won the battle.

After the battle, your fellow warriors carry you home on a litter. Your arm will take weeks to heal, and it will never be as strong as before. Your days as a warrior are over, but you will lead a rewarding life as the emperor's favourite landscape gardener. Your gardens become famous and bring pleasure to all who see them.

THE END

To follow another path, turn to page 11.
To read the conclusion, turn to page 101.

Despite the pain, you strike out again. But your arm is weak. You are bleeding heavily and you fall to the ground. The battle continues around you. You no longer hear the war cries as the life drains out of you. You focus instead on the swirl of bright colours from tribal banners, decorated cloaks, and the painted faces of warriors. Then you close your eyes for the last time. Your death on the battlefield will bring you honour.

THE END

To follow another path, turn to page 11.
To read the conclusion, turn to page 101.

"Let's wait," you say. "Help me to my room."

Luc does his best to help you. He brings food and drink and makes excuses so that no one misses you.

But by the next day, you have developed a fever. Your leg is swollen and hot, and you moan with pain. Finally your friend calls a priest.

The priest prays over you and offers various medicines, but the leg gets worse. Despite their best efforts, the healers cannot help you. You die on a mat in your room at school, never having experienced the excitement of battle.

65

THE END

To follow another path, turn to page 11.
To read the conclusion, turn to page 101.

"Go ahead and get help," you moan.

Luc finds a priest who is also a healer. The priest applies a healing salve, splints the leg, and carries you to your room. Unfortunately, the leg does not heal well. You walk with a limp, and you can no longer run.

"You'll never be a warrior," Father says, disappointment clouding his face. "This accident must be a sign from the gods. You will prove yourself in other ways."

You return to the palace gardens and study with the royal landscape gardener. Someday you will be in charge of designing the emperor's gardens.

Crops and gardens were
difficult to grow on the
swampy island and were
therefore highly valued.

THE END

To follow another path, turn to page 11.
To read the conclusion, turn to page 101.

You hesitate at first. When the battle begins, the highest-ranking warriors enter the battlefield first. Eagle and Jaguar knights follow them. Finally it is your turn, and you feel ready to enter the battle.

Successful, costumed warriors entered the battle before lower ranking warriors.

The battlefield is strewn with bodies. You crouch low and approach a warrior who looks to be about your age. You jab at him with your spear. He jabs back, but his aim is better than yours. He plunges the spear into your thigh.

You look down to see blood spurting from your leg. You grab the wound, but cannot stop the bleeding. You collapse on the battlefield, the life quickly draining from your body. It is a noble death. Your last thoughts are hopeful ones. You imagine yourself as a hummingbird living forever, favoured by the gods.

THE END

To follow another path, turn to page 11.
To read the conclusion, turn to page 101.

Montezuma II greeted Hernán Cortés in Tenochtitlan.

CHAPTER 4

Spanish page

You are 12 years old. Your family moved from Spain to the Spanish colony of Cuba a year ago so your father could work for the governor. One day your father announces that he has found a position for you as a page. "Hernán Cortés is leading an expedition to New Spain. You will go with him."

On 19 February 1519, you leave Cuba with Cortés. He brings 11 ships, 508 soldiers, 17 horses, and several large mastiff dogs. There are weapons, too – cannons and guns. Will there be trouble ahead?

Turn the page.

You do whatever Cortés asks – fetch supplies, polish his boots, and check on the horses. You stay on the ship when Cortés goes ashore at Cozumel, where many Tabascan people live. He returns with gifts from the Tabascans, including several female slaves.

Cortés orders the ships to head northwest. "We're going to find gold," he says.

Even before you reach shore, royal visitors arrive bearing more gifts. They speak an unfamiliar language. But one of the Tabascan slaves understands them. "They are Aztec nobles," she says. "The great emperor Montezuma II sent them."

Cortés' eyes sparkle with pleasure as he admires the jewellery, cloaks, and feather work they've brought. He looks at the young slave girl and asks her name. "Malinche," she replies shyly.

From that moment on, Malinche remains at Cortés' side to translate the words of the Aztec leaders. It's not easy. She translates the Nahuatl language of the Aztecs into the Mayan language. Then a Mayan-speaking priest named Aguilar translates it into Spanish. But Malinche is clever and quickly learns Spanish. Soon Aguilar no longer needs to translate.

When Montezuma's ambassadors return, they bring more gifts of gold. "Take these gifts and go," they say. But Cortés has no intention of leaving. He plans to find Montezuma's city of gold.

It takes three months of travel through mountain passes to reach the capital city of Tenochtitlan. At last you see it in the valley below. You enter the city on one of three causeways – raised paths across the lake.

Turn the page.

The great Montezuma climbs out of a golden litter carried by servants. He's wearing a cloak embroidered with golden threads and an enormous feathered headdress. After the leaders exchange greetings, Montezuma takes Cortés to the Palace Axayacatl, the former home of Montezuma's father. It's the most elegant building you've ever seen. It's large enough for Cortés and all his men to stay there.

The next afternoon Montezuma invites Cortés to visit his palace. Malinche will serve as translator. You can go if you want.

74

➤To go to Montezuma's palace, go to page **75**.
➤To wait at the Palace Axayacatl, turn to page **78**.

You follow Cortés and Malinche to Montezuma's palace. The palace's long hallways lead to hundreds of rooms grouped around three huge courtyards. He shows you the fabulous grounds and the rare animals in the zoo.

On the return to Palace Axayacatl, you overhear Cortés speaking with his officers. "The men are getting restless," a captain says.

"This place is dangerous," says another. "We are trapped on an island. Montezuma could order us all killed."

"Don't worry. I will soon take him prisoner," says Cortés.

The next afternoon Cortés, Malinche, the captains, and 30 well-armed soldiers return to Montezuma's palace. You go along.

Turn the page.

You have begun to learn a few words of Nahuatl, the Aztec language. Knowing the language is useful, especially when you meet Montezuma or his warriors.

You're surprised when Cortés accuses Montezuma of attacking the Spanish settlement of Veracruz on the coast. "I have no desire to start a war or to destroy Tenochtitlan. Everything will be forgiven, if you come with us. You will be as well served and attended as in your own palace," Cortés tells him.

At first, Montezuma protests. After several hours of argument, he agrees to go, but not as a prisoner. He informs his people that he is going to stay with Cortés to learn more about the Spanish and their ways. Only then does the mighty emperor call for his royal litter and ride to the Palace Axayacatl with Cortés.

For the next five months, Montezuma rules his people from Axayacatl. But there is no doubt he is a prisoner. Anyone wishing to speak to Montezuma must get permission from Cortés.

One day Malinche overhears Montezuma planning a revolt with his military advisers. She tells Cortés. When Cortés confronts Montezuma, the Aztec leader confesses. He adds that his runners saw 18 Spanish warships anchored off the coast at Veracruz. The ships belong to Diego de Velázquez, the governor of Cuba. Pánfilo de Narváez is in command. He and Velázquez plan to challenge Cortés over Aztec gold.

Cortés splits his forces. Some will remain in Tenochtitlan guarding Montezuma. The rest will go with Cortés to confront Narváez.

➤To go with Cortés, turn to page **82**.
➤To stay in Tenochtitlan, turn to page **83**.

You have work to do organizing supplies, so you stay at the palace. When Cortés returns, he brings word that Montezuma has given permission for the Spanish to roam the city freely. You've learned some Nahuatl by listening to Malinche and the servants. Perhaps it is time to explore the city on your own.

You go to the marketplace. Thousands of shoppers barter for goods. Canoes shuttle back and forth from one shore to the other, bringing fruits and vegetables to market. One farmer carries dozens of purple flowers from his flat-bottomed canoe to a flower vendor's stall.

Beyond the marketplace, you notice that the homes become smaller. Women sit in the courtyards visiting and caring for children. Canals allow canoes to travel throughout the city. Boards laid from one side to the other form bridges so you can walk over the canals.

When you reach the lakeshore, you see several of the flat-bottomed canoes pulled up at the water's edge. You are tempted to borrow one and try rowing around the lake. Is anyone watching?

➻To return to the palace, turn to page **80**.

➻To take a canoe, turn to page **92**.

"Where have you been?" one of the officers asks back at the palace. "While you were out, Cortés has taken Montezuma prisoner."

"Prisoner?"

"Yes. We feared an uprising of the Aztecs. We feel trapped on this island. Cortés convinced Montezuma to come here so we can keep an eye on him."

Cortés took Montezuma prisoner in 1520.

Weeks pass. You spend time with Montezuma. He seems to enjoy your company. You are one of the few Spanish who can speak Nahuatl.

One day Cortés rushes into Montezuma's chambers. "Out, boy!" he says.

You later learn that Montezuma and his nobles had been planning a revolt. Montezuma also told Cortés that Diego de Velázquez, the governor of Cuba, was planning to challenge Cortés. At first Velázquez had supported Cortés, but now he wanted the gold for himself.

Cortés tells his troops, "Get ready to march!" When you begin packing supplies, he takes you aside and orders you to remain in Tenochtitlan. Malinche is going with him. Someone who speaks Nahuatl must stay behind.

Turn to page 83.

You go with Cortés and 350 soldiers to confront Narváez. Just outside the city of Tlaxcala, you meet Andrés de Duero, a friend of Cortés who had helped him plan the expedition. Duero is Governor Velázquez's secretary.

Cortés offers Duero and his soldiers gifts of gold if they will desert Velázquez. The men accept his offer and tell Cortés the exact location of Narváez and his men.

Even though it's pouring rain and the ground is slick with mud, Cortés leads his men on. "We attack tonight," he says. He orders Malinche to wait in a ravine along with the food and equipment.

→To go with Malinche, turn to page 89.

→To remain with Cortés, turn to page 98.

You stay at the palace. Captain Alvarado is in charge. Cortés has left 120 men to guard the city and the emperor.

The big Festival of Toxcatl is about to begin. Montezuma asks Alvarado to allow the people to celebrate. The festival occurs every May to honour the Aztec god Tezcatlipoca. It's a time of praying for rain to fill the rivers and nourish the crops. It's also a time of human sacrifices. But Montezuma knows that Cortés does not approve of human sacrifice. If Alvarado forbids the celebration, Montezuma fears the people will rebel.

"There will be no sacrifices," Montezuma promises Alvarado.

Turn the page.

As you walk around the city with Alvarado, you see captives held in cages near the temple. One of the Aztec statues holds a paper banner drenched in blood. Despite Montezuma's promises, it looks as if the priests are planning human sacrifices. Alvarado is worried but agrees to allow the celebration.

On the fourth day of the celebration, Alvarado and his soldiers gather weapons and put on their armour. "What's happening?" you ask.

"Tonight is the Serpent Dance at the Patio of Dances," one soldier says. "The captain has heard rumours that the Aztecs are planning a revolt."

"Sixty men will guard the palace," another soldier says. "Sixty will go with Alvarado." You are not a fighter, but you could go along and help fire the cannons.

→To go to the Patio of Dances, go to page 85.
→To stay and guard the palace, turn to page 86.

You follow the soldiers to the Patio of Dances. Drums beat, flutes play, and about 500 dancers sway. You stand near one of the gates as hundreds of Aztec nobles and warriors file into the patio. Spanish soldiers surround the patio.

Suddenly the Spanish soldiers close the gates, trapping everyone inside. The soldiers run into the crowd with their swords, killing everyone they meet. The crowd panics. They are unarmed. It's a massacre! The brilliant green quetzal feathers on the dancers' costumes turn red with blood. You are too sickened to move.

A soldier pushes you aside. "Go!" he yells.

Turn to page **95**.

You stay at the palace. Suddenly, screams pierce the night. It's coming from the Patio of Dances. "What's happening?" The screaming turns to wailing, and the entire city seems to be at the palace gates.

"We're under siege," an officer says. "The Aztecs are attacking."

"Attacking?" you ask, but the soldiers are too busy fighting to answer. Later, you learn that Alvarado and his men attacked first at the Patio of Dances. Thousands of Aztecs died.

For days, Aztec warriors storm the palace gates. You run out of food, and the water is nearly gone. Alvarado sends a messenger under cover of darkness to find Cortés and bring him back. Cortés arrives just in time and manages to create a temporary truce.

But Montezuma is a defeated man. Alvarado has placed him in leg irons. He is no longer an impressive king – only a captive. His gold belongs to the Spanish, and soon his city will too. You try to comfort the emperor, but it's useless. Even you can see that the day will soon come when the Aztecs and Spanish fight to the death.

On 1 July 1520, Cortés insists that Montezuma go to the rooftop of the palace to talk to his people. But who can hear him over the Aztec drumming and stone throwing? Even Montezuma is not safe. A rock hits him on the head. Had the stone thrower meant to hit a Spanish soldier? Probably. But it is Montezuma who falls.

Turn the page.

"Montezuma!" you cry as the soldiers carry him to safety. He survives for three days but refuses the food and drink you offer. When Montezuma dies, you feel as if you have lost a favourite uncle.

Within a year, the empire collapses. Cortés is in charge now. As the work of rebuilding begins, Cortés sends another treasure shipment to Spain.

Montezuma was fatally injured on the rooftop of the Palace Axayacatl.

➤To sail to Spain with the gold, turn to page **93**.

➤To remain in Mexico, turn to page **94**.

It's a relief when one of the officers comes to get you and Malinche. "The battle is over," he says. "Narváez surrendered."

You barely reach Cortés when a messenger arrives. "You are needed at Tenochtitlan," he says. "Captain Alvarado feared a revolt, so he attacked the Aztecs during the ceremony. Thousands died. Alvarado and his men are trapped in the palace without food or water."

Cortés races to Tenochtitlan. It's like a ghost town. The people have gone into hiding. Alvarado's men are starving after days without food. They cheer when Cortés arrives.

Cortés cannot persuade Montezuma to open the markets to get his soldiers food. However, Montezuma tricks Cortés into believing that Montezuma's brother Cuitláhuac, who is also a prisoner, can help.

Turn the page.

As soon as Cortés releases him, Cuitláhuac calls in warriors from distant cities and villages. The next morning, they begin attacking the Palace Axayacatl, where you are staying.

The Aztec war cries frighten you. Even worse, the Aztecs throw stones over the palace walls. It's as if stones are raining from the sky. The Aztecs send flaming arrows into the courtyard too.

Cortés orders the cannons fired. His crossbowmen send volleys of arrows at the enemy, but still the fighting continues. A warrior rushes through the gate towards Cortés and attacks him. Cortés slumps against the wall.

➤To call for help, go to page **91**.

➤To rush to Cortés' aid, turn to page **97**.

You report what you've seen to one of Cortés' captains. He sends two soldiers to help Cortés to safety. The conquistador is bleeding. But his wounds are not serious. As soon as you bandage him, he rushes back to the battle.

The fighting continues throughout the next day, but you barely know what's happening. At last an officer tells you, "We leave at midnight for Tlaxcala. We'll take as much gold as we can. Fill your pockets."

But Cortés warns, "Better not to overload yourselves. He who travels safest in the dark night travels lightest."

→To carry two bags of gold, turn to page **96**.

→To take only one gold necklace, turn to page **99**.

You push the canoe into the water and begin to row. The lake is huge. You find that rowing is hard work. You're getting very tired. The sun is beginning to set. You are almost to the other side when you hear a noise. Is that an enemy lying in wait? Fear makes you move quickly. You turn the boat around and begin rowing in the other direction. But your arms are weak and shaky, and you're confused in the dark.

Another noise frightens you, and when you jump, the boat rocks. You lose your balance and tumble into the lake. "Help!" you cry as you sink beneath the water. You cannot swim. Your last thoughts are of your family as you drown in Lake Texcoco.

THE END

To follow another path, turn to page 11.
To read the conclusion, turn to page 101.

92

You volunteer to go along. It will be good to see your relatives still living in Spain.

"Guard my gold," Cortés says as you leave. You fully intend to do so. But just before you reach Spain, French pirates attack the ship.

You reach for a sword to protect the gold. But before you pick it up, one of the pirates pushes the point of his weapon into your chest. He tosses you overboard. You sink to the bottom of the sea, another victim of the quest for Aztec gold.

93

THE END

To follow another path, turn to page 11.
To read the conclusion, turn to page 101.

You like Mexico. It's your home now.

Spain's King Charles names Cortés governor and captain-general of New Spain. Cortés is responsible for rebuilding the city and exploring other lands in America. He sends troops to Guatemala and Honduras. You remain at his side and become an important member of his household. You advise him on matters related to his household and day-to-day life in Tenochtitlan, now renamed Mexico City.

In a few years, you marry an Aztec woman and raise several children. They grow up speaking both Spanish and the Aztec language of Nahuatl.

94

THE END

To follow another path, turn to page 11.
To read the conclusion, turn to page 101.

You run and hide in a dark alley. Wails echo through the city. A loud voice begins to call, "Mexicanos, come running! The strangers have murdered our people!"

Warriors rush from their homes armed with shields and spears. You huddle against a hut, trying to disappear. But a boy finds you there. His yell brings others who hit you with sticks, tie you up, and drag you to the temple. You're killed quickly by a priest's knife, and your heart is offered to the gods.

THE END

To follow another path, turn to page 11.
To read the conclusion, turn to page 101.

You grab several bags of gold. At least you'll have no money problems in the future. But the gold is heavy, and you fall far behind the others. Suddenly out of the darkness appears a painted warrior. He swings his weapon at you, catching you in the knee. You fall to the ground. As you struggle to get up, the warrior drives his spear into your chest. You die instantly.

The Aztecs made gold, stone, and turquoise statues of the fire god Xiuhtecuhtli.

THE END

To follow another path, turn to page 11.
To read the conclusion, turn to page 101.

You rush to Cortés. So does Captain Alvarado. "Help me get him inside," Alvarado says.

As you reach out to help Cortés, a rock smashes into your head. You slump to the ground. Feeling your head, you discover it is bleeding. You're dizzy and your legs don't work. The last thing you see before you die is Captain Alvarado helping Cortés to safety.

THE END

To follow another path, turn to page 11.
To read the conclusion, turn to page 101.

When fighting begins, you realize that you should have gone with Malinche. If you had, you'd be safe. Cortés is on horseback leading his troops. You are on foot and without a weapon. Your only hope is to run into the forest and hide. But as you run, something heavy hits your head. It knocks you to the ground.

You feel sick when you stand up, but you keep walking. Getting to safety drives you forward. One of Cortés' soldiers finds you staggering alone.

"What happened?" he asks.

"My head," you moan.

"Lie down," he says. "You'll be fine after you rest." But you're not. The pain in your head increases. By morning you are dead from a fractured skull.

THE END

To follow another path, turn to page 11.
To read the conclusion, turn to page 101.

It is dark when you slip the necklace around your neck and follow the guards past the Pyramid of the Sun. When you reach the giant causeway at Tacuba, soldiers must repair damaged sections of the bridge so that you can cross. You're nearly across when an Aztec woman suddenly yells, "Mexicanos! Come running! Our enemies are escaping!"

You escape the island just before canoes full of Aztec warriors enter the water. You huddle in safety with Malinche and the priests. Cortés leads his troops into battle. Nearly 600 of his men die that night. So do hundreds of Aztecs.

After the battle, you begin the march to the friendly city of Tlaxcala, 80 kilometres (50 miles) away. Cortés is already making plans to retake Tenochtitlan.

THE END

To follow another path, turn to page 11.
To read the conclusion, turn to page 101.

Today a plaza in Mexico City stands near the ruins of Tenochtitlan.

CHAPTER 5

The end of an empire

Hernán Cortés, the Spanish conquistador, not only ended the reign of the Aztec rulers, but he also destroyed their great city. Thousands of Tenochtitlan's people died in the final battles.

Montezuma died too. The Spanish believed that he died of a head wound caused by rocks the Aztecs threw at Spanish soldiers. The Aztecs, however, claimed that the Spanish killed him. The survivors saw Spanish soldiers destroy their homes, topple their pyramids, and steal their remaining treasures.

As terrible as the fighting was, a worse enemy was looming. The Spanish had brought the deadly smallpox with them. The Aztecs had no resistance to the disease, and they died by the thousands. In some areas, half of the people died of smallpox. Many others starved to death, too sick to find food. Cuitláhuac, who became emperor after Montezuma II, died of smallpox on 4 December 1520.

Cuauhtémoc, nephew of Cuitláhuac and Montezuma, became the last emperor of the Aztecs. Cortés and his soldiers conquered the city a final time in 1521. The people fled. The city was destroyed.

Much of the Aztec gold was lost. In the last days of the Empire, Aztec warriors dumped baskets of gold into Lake Texcoco. The gold Cortés found was melted down and sent to Spain. But much of it never arrived. Some loads were lost at sea, and French pirates took the rest.

The Spanish were horrified by the Aztec practice of human sacrifice. Cortés and his men watched captives taken to the top of a pyramid and forced onto a stone table. The Aztecs believed that blood sacrifices convinced the gods to provide for them. While four priests held the captive down, another pierced his chest with a sharp knife and removed the heart. The priest then held the heart in the air as an offering to the gods.

To Cortés' horror, some of his own men became victims of sacrifice after battles with Aztec warriors. Stopping this practice became one of his goals. Cortés set up Roman Catholic shrines. Spanish priests baptized natives in every conquered town or city. After the conquest Catholic priests established churches and schools to convert the natives. Today most Mexicans practise the Roman Catholic faith.

Some Catholic priests realized that valuable Aztec knowledge had been lost. They gathered artists and storytellers to create books of drawings about their life in the time before Cortés arrived. Much of what we now know about the Aztecs comes from these books.

More than 1 million people in Mexico still speak the Nahuatl language. Tourists who visit Mexico can tour the ruins of Aztec pyramids and temples or take a boat ride on canals dug by Aztec farmers.

Mexico gave us tortillas, tamales, and tomatoes, as well as hot cocoa. Modern doctors use several Aztec medicines to treat diseases. Aztec artists created beautiful works of art and woven cloth. The red dye that the Aztecs made from the cochineal bugs is still used. Even though the Aztec Empire ended 400 years ago, it continues to influence our daily lives.

Time line

AD 1100 – The Aztecs leave their home in Aztlan.

1100–1200s – The Aztecs reach central Mexico and establish city-states in the valleys and plains surrounding the Valley of Mexico.

1325 – The city of Tenochtitlan is founded on an island in Lake Texcoco in the Valley of Mexico.

1325–1428 – The Aztecs construct a dyke and canal system in Tenochtitlan; Texcoco and Tlacopan join with Tenochtitlan to form the Triple Alliance; Acamapichtli becomes the first king of the Aztec Empire.

1390 – Construction of Templo Mayor, the major pyramid, begins in Tenochtitlan.

1440 – Montezuma I begins a 28-year reign.

1450–1452 – A severe drought destroys the harvest, causing thousands of people to starve.

1473 – The Aztecs conquer Tlatelolco, a neighbouring city.

1502 – Montezuma II, the most well-known Aztec king, is crowned.

1519 – Hernán Cortés arrives on the coast of Mexico in March; he establishes Veracruz; he reaches Tenochtitlan in November and enters the city as a guest of Montezuma.

1520 – Cortés begins an assault on the Aztec Empire; Montezuma dies; the next emperor, Cuitláhuac, drives the Spanish out of the city before dying of smallpox.

1521 – Spanish and Tlaxcalans attack Tenochtitlan and conquer the city; the last emperor, Cuauhtémoc, surrenders to Cortés on 13 August.

1522 – The Spanish rebuild Tenochtitlan as Mexico City, capital of New Spain; Cortés becomes the governor of New Spain.

OTHER PATHS TO EXPLORE

In this book you've seen how the events of the past look different from three points of view. Perspectives on history are as varied as the people who lived it. Seeing history from many points of view is an important part of understanding it.

Here are some ideas for other points of view to explore:

- The Aztec city-states were always at war with neighbouring city-states. The winner demanded victims for sacrifice from these towns. How would life change if you lived in constant fear of being sacrificed?

- Soldiers, sailors, and servants chose to go to the Americas with the conquistadors. If you were living then, would you have been likely to go?

- Imagine you lived in Tenochtitlan at the time of the conquest. People from a distant country move in and destroy your home. They refuse to allow you to practise your religion. Would you be quick to change or would you cling to your old ways as long as possible?

READ MORE

The Aztecs (Ancient People and Places), Richard F Townsend (Thames and Hudson Ltd, 2010)

Aztecs (Eyewitness Project Books) (DK, 2011)

Hands on History: Aztecs: Dress, eat, write and play just like the Aztecs, Fiona Macdonald (QED Publishing, 2011)

Aztec, Inca and Maya, Elizabeth Baquedano (DK, 2011)

INTERNET SITES

Visit these websites to find out more about the Aztecs:

www.bbc.co.uk/education/topics/zvjqtfr

www.kidskonnect.com/subjectindex/16-educational/
history/250-ancient-aztec.html

www.socialstudiesforkids.com/subjects/aztec.htm

GLOSSARY

ambassador – government official who represents his or her country

conquistador – military leader in the Spanish conquest of North and South America during the 1500s

convert – to change from one religion or faith to another

elite – group of people who have special advantages or talents

embroidery – form of sewing used to sew pictures or designs on cloth

litter – stretcher for carrying a wounded person

maguey – type of agave plant with spines

ochre – yellow or reddish-yellow iron ore or other earth materials used to colour something

quetzal – red and green bird that is the national bird of Guatemala

salve – medicine or lotion that relieves pain and helps heal wounds or burns

truce – agreement to stop fighting in a war

turquoise – blue-green gemstone

BIBLIOGRAPHY

Boone, Elizabeth Hill. *The Aztec World.* Washington, D.C.: Smithsonian Books, 1994.

Carrasco, Davíd. *Daily Life of The Aztecs: People of the Sun and Earth.* Westport, Conn.: Greenwood Press, 1998.

Clendinnen, Inga. *Aztecs.* New York: Cambridge U.P., 1991.

Levy, Buddy. *Conquistador: Hernán Cortés, King Montezuma, and the Last Stand of the Aztecs.* New York: Bantam, 2008.

Marks, Richard Lee. *Cortés: The Great Adventurer and the Fate of Aztec Mexico.* New York: Alfred A. Knopf, 1993.

Marrin, Albert. *Aztecs and Spaniards: Cortés and the Conquest of Mexico.* New York: Atheneum, 1986.

Smith, Michael E. *The Aztecs.* Oxford: Blackwell, 1996.

Teresi, Dick. *Lost Discoveries: The Ancient Roots of Modern Science—from the Babylonians to the Maya.* New York: Simon & Schuster, 2002.

Townsend, Richard F. *The Aztecs.* London: Thames & Hudson, 1992.

Van Tuerenhout, Dirk T. *The Aztecs: New Perspectives.* Santa Barbara, Calif.: ABC-CLIO, 2005.

INDEX